CATH KIDSTON
VINTAGE STYLE

A NEW APPROACH TO HOME DECORATING

CATH KIDSTON
VINTAGE STYLE

PHOTOGRAPHS   PIA TRYDE

EBURY PRESS
LONDON

To my family

First published in 1999

5 7 9 10 8 6

Text © 1999 Cath Kidston
Photographs © 1999 Pia Tryde

First published in the United Kingdom in 1999 by Ebury Press
Random House, 20 Vauxhall Bridge Road, London SW1V 2SA

Random House Australia (Pty) Limited
20 Alfred Street, Milsons Point, Sydney, New South Wales 2061, Australia

Random House New Zealand Limited
18 Poland Road, Glenfield, Auckland 10, New Zealand

Random House South Africa (Pty) Limited
Endulini, 5a Jubilee Road, Parktown 2193, South Africa

Random House UK Limited Reg. No. 954009

A CIP catalogue record for this book is available from the British Library.

ISBN 0 09 186549 2

DESIGNER **GEORGINA RHODES**
PROJECT EDITOR **EMMA CALLERY**

Printed and bound in Singapore by Tien Wah Press

contents

introduction

RIGHT

At home. By chance
I am dressed to match
my pink and white
sitting room!

My fascination with interior design began at a very early age. For some strange reason I can recollect every inch of my childhood home, my best friend's bedroom curtains, or the colour of a certain armchair. While I am hopeless at remembering all sorts of important things, such as telephone numbers or shopping lists, I can recollect an exact fabric or wallpaper that I may not have seen for fifteen years. I am not quite sure how my obsession began.

While both my parents were very interested in the decoration of our house and took a good deal of trouble in making it pretty, once they had furnished the rooms and hung the curtains, they let the place be. The emphasis was very much on it being a comfortable family home with the dogs allowed to sit on the sofa and even our donkey coming into the sitting room for tea and chocolate biscuits. It was not consciously a haven of interior design.

Early experiments

I probably spent most of my childhood outdoors on a pony, but the thing I remember most is the excitement of choosing my own curtains for the first time and the fun I had constantly rearranging my bedroom furniture. Since then I have spent quite a few years involved in interior design.

I have seen all sorts of trends come and go; from stripped pine and peach stippled walls to grand swags and tails. My own taste has changed and adapted over this time, but somehow the thing that has most influenced me and I have repeatedly come back to are the prints and fabrics of my childhood. I was contemplating this one day as I sat at home wading through piles of old books and magazines. I wanted to start my own interior design shop at the time but needed some sort of push to give me the confidence to do so. I felt there had to be a way of combining these old designs into contemporary decorating. The bold cabbage rose curtains I had kept all those years or that lilac chintz I had found at auction looked far fresher to me than anything that was on the market. Then I came across the most wonderful photograph of a bathroom. It was a complete inspiration to me. The walls were the palest duck egg blue paint, the floor plain cork tiling. The furniture was simple and practical, too. A large laundry cupboard on the back wall, a simple table and chair by the bath – and all painted shiny white. A set of classic Redouté rose prints hung on the wall and a sheepskin mat lay by the bath. But what made the room was the completely unexpected, rather eccentric, splash of cabbage rose wallpaper covering the panels

of the bath. This room must have been decorated about thirty years ago and yet it had a freshness, originality and honesty about it that is hard to find today.

Creating my shop

Inspired by this photograph I set about starting my own business. The first thing I did was to invest half of my minuscule budget in developing my own cabbage print wallpaper. I chose classic red roses with dark green leaves on a fresh white background, just like the panel around the old bath tub. I then combed the junk shops and markets for furniture and vintage fabrics.

I was encouraged at how easy it was to find handsome pieces of furniture for very little money. Most of them needed a coat of paint, but were easily transformed. The wallpaper was perfect for lining the cupboards and drawers and it is amazing what a difference a new set of handles can make.

The biggest surprise of all, though, was the availability of the old fabrics. I wasn't interested in grand silk damask or French toile de jouy – instead, I focused on finding the cheerful floral prints of my childhood. It was simply a question of rummaging around at flea markets or sale rooms rather than going to smart antique shops, but there was plenty to be found.

LEFT

An old eiderdown gets a new lease of life with a paisely loose cover. The edges are trimmed in taffetta, an idea copied from the original quilt.

OPPOSITE

The colours of this oil painting inspired the colour scheme for my bedroom.

*I bought these
wire shelves from
a car boot sale with
no particular use
in mind. But they
have worked out as
ideal storage for
the stationery in
my office.*

14

The thing that had struck me most about the bathroom picture had been the unexpected use of the floral paper on the side of the bath. The element of surprise appealed to me in particular and triggered my imagination. I loved the idea of using my favourite old chintz for a laundry bag instead of curtain, or that leftover piece of striped linen for perhaps a roller towel.

So I started to turn these ideas into products for my shop. Ironing board covers made from lengths of vintage dress fabric were the first experiment, and I was so encouraged by their popularity that other items soon followed.

Decorating my home

Around this time I moved house and it was the perfect opportunity to experiment with these ideas at home. I painted the entire place white from top to toe in order to move in with a clean slate and slowly began the decorating.

I have gathered quite a lot of furniture and pictures over the years and many of these objects are of great sentimental value. Some things I collected a while ago and are no longer fashionable but I wanted to try and use most of what I had. It turned out that this actually helped rather than restrained the decorating. For example, a bright pink and yellow oil painting by my great aunt inspired the colours for my sitting room, and an old skipping rope with red and torquoise paint gave me the idea of adding blue to my red and white kitchen. The colour scheme of my lilac and green bedroom also stemmed from some paintings I had inherited.

Once I had decided on the basic idea for each room I could begin to decorate. For instance, in my kitchen I felt safe with the idea of ordering a bright blue cooker and knew that I could then collect fabrics for tablecloths, seat cushions and even the tea towels. Gradually I began to build each room, buying things as I came across them in junk shops and markets. Several years have now passed and although the house has had a lived-in feel for some time, the decoration continues to evolve. I still love combing the junk shops and markets and never know what I will find next. Also, as I now have a much wider collection of my own fabrics and wallpapers in my shop, I can use these at home. I love to combine them with the old fabrics and there is nothing like finding a wonderful old pair of rosy curtains at a boot sale.

This book is really an illustration of how, with my love of textiles and everday household objects, I have developed a certain style of decorating. I am sure my taste will change again with time, but my love of floral chintz will always remain.

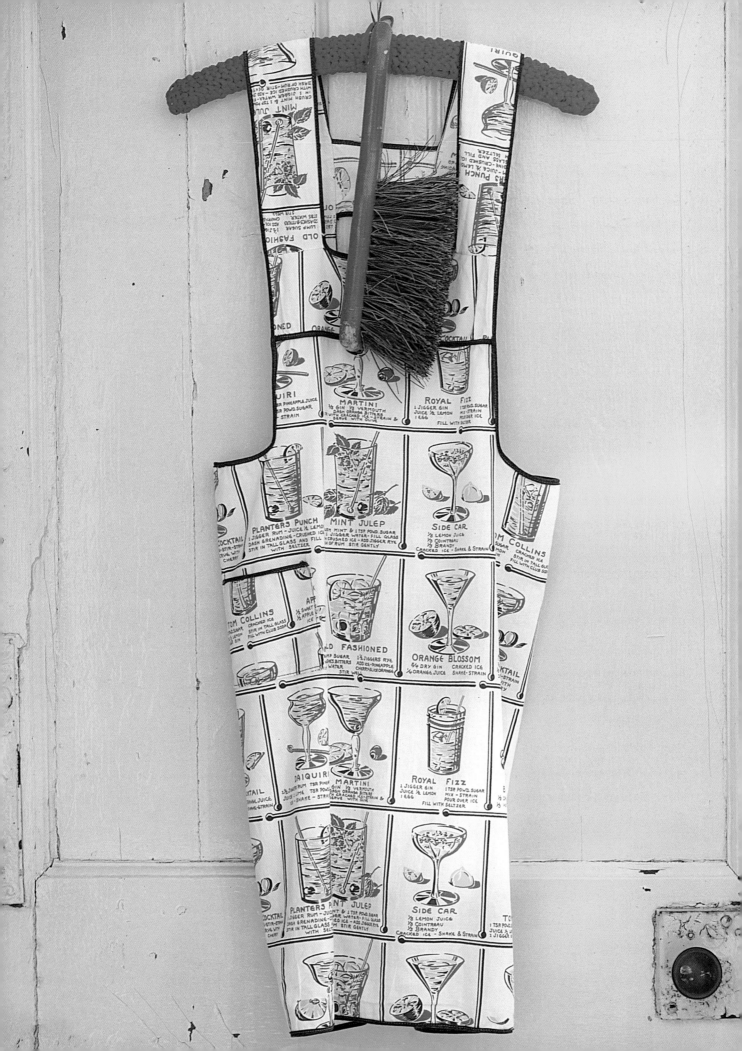

the kitchen

the kitchen

The kitchen really is the heart of our house. More time is spent chatting around the kitchen table than anywhere else and besides cooking and eating it is used as the main congregating area throughout the day for the family. In London we have opened up the entire basement area to form a large kitchen. The cooking is at one end, the table in the middle and a sitting area with a fireplace and television at the far end. At first glance, this is a fantastic room, but in practice it has many drawbacks. We seem to spend our entire time in the basement, which is rather dark, and never use our sitting room on the ground floor. Added to this, the room is also used as a playroom, so it is forever strewn with toys, newspapers and clutter. When we bought our house in the country I made sure we arranged the living space in a much more segregated way and now we spread ourselves throughout the house.

Before we moved in I painted the entire interior white in order to start with a clean slate. I didn't want to make any hurried decisions and as time goes by I am gradually painting a few of the rooms in different colours. Much of the house will remain white, the kitchen in particular, as I like the versatility that this gives me in decorating the rest of the room. After the dark basement kitchen, I wanted to keep the new one as light as possible and I didn't want to use a colour that would be tying in years to come. Kitchens are the one room in the house that need to be repainted fairly regularly, so it also seemed the most practical solution as it is simple to add a fresh coat of white paint. The only thing that guided me in choosing the other colours for the room was that over the years I have collected an enormous amount of red and white kitchenware. There is everything from striped storage jars to chequered enamel pans, egg cups, soup ladles and mugs. I knew I wanted to use this all again but I also wanted a change from my previous red and white kitchen so have introduced blue as well. Once I had decided on these colours, the basis of the room was set.

Making changes

First of all I was lucky enough to find a new cooker that was available in a wonderful blue enamel. It heats up in the same way as an old-fashioned range to keep the kitchen cosy in the winter and is the focal point of the room. A plain chimney breast was then built around the cooker with a simple mantel shelf over the top to disguise the extractor. To complete the space, I then tiled behind the cooker with plain white tiles.

We had inherited kitchen cupboards and I was loathe to throw them all away as they

These storage bags are
great for keeping rice
and lentils neat and
tidy. They can be hung
from hooks if you are
short of shelf space.

19

ABOVE

This roller towel was made from a vintage linen lined with a light white towelling fabric. These bold 1950s floral prints can look great when used sparingly against a stark white background in a contemporary setting.

were well built. Overhead units can be rather oppressive so I replaced them with open shelves right up to the ceiling. These are excellent for storage jars and a place to hook up numerous cups and mugs. I keep half a dozen of our everyday glasses and plates on the shelves just above the washing machine, which is so much easier than having to put them away on a daily basis. The lower units originally had rather fussy doors but now they have been re-faced with simple panels painted with a fresh white gloss. I was lucky enough to inherit an old flagstone floor, which scrubbed up very well, so the basis of the room is really very simple.

The focal point

The main focus of the room is a big kitchen table. A set of new kitchen chairs are grouped around the pine table, and I have painted them in a strong red paint to match the kitchenware. I had a really pretty set of old kitchen chairs but they were very fragile and were always having to be repaired. The advantage of the new chairs is they are robust enough to take the wear and tear of kitchen life. They are extremely comfortable and the squab seats are easy to take off and wash. If I get bored with the red paint, it would be easy to alter them to a different colour. I have covered the seat cushions in a red and white

the kitchen

RIGHT

This strawberry print adds a splash of colour in my all-white kitchen.

OPPOSITE

These favourite cook books are covered in oilcloth or wallpaper to protect them from greasy fingers!

checked cotton on one side and a vintage print on the other so they can be swapped around if I feel like a change.

I am still looking for a large enough table for the room. To improvise, a large piece of wood from a timber merchant is laid over the existing table, which is much too small. I did this as an emergency over Christmas when we had a house full and it may stay like this for years. With a tablecloth thrown over the top no one need ever be any the wiser. Changing the cloths really alters the feel of a room and I have collected all sorts over the years.

Fabrics add colour

Vintage fabrics can make great tablecloths and if there are no other patterns in a room, big bold floral prints can look great on a table. It is possible to find them already made into curtains and so long as they are washable cotton and not interlined they are easy to convert. They are often the right size for a 180 cm (6 ft) table and it is usually a case of just unpicking the heading tape and hemming along one end. Tablecloths that are too small can be bordered in either gingham or plain white linen to fit.

We have a table in the hall, which can be used for a dining room, but we tend to eat in the kitchen when we entertain. It is only once in a while for some special reason that we set

the kitchen

RIGHT

This vintage floral tablecloth has been extended with a wide white linen border. The edges are then finished off in a contrasting bias binding.

OPPOSITE

Herbs and pulses sit in bags in my store cupboard. They are made from various leftover scraps of tickings and ginghams and then labelled with a marker pen.

OVERLEAF

Variations of the same print are used to cover these painted antique Swedish chairs.

up the hall for eating. Instead, if I need to make the kitchen look a bit smarter in the evening, I use a white tablecloth. Vintage French linen sheets are wonderful for this purpose as they have such a rustic quality. They also dye beautifully in the washing machine to make coloured cloths. They are quite readily available in antique shops and markets and are very good value compared to traditional damask cloths.

In addition to tablecloths and napkins, tea towels bring colour and interest to a kitchen. As mine live on the cooker they are always on full display, so I try to have cloths that look cheerful in the room. I love the old floral towels from the 1950s, which are quite hard to find and sometimes have frayed edges. This can be remedied by trimming off the ends and adding a border such as a strip of crocheted lace. It is easy to make your own by simply hemming rectangles of printed linen. Edging the cloths with bias binding, as with the napkins, also looks good.

One of my favourite things in the kitchen is an old floral roller towel. We have a scullery and store room off the kitchen which has a small sink. The roller towel is made from a bright piece of floral linen and hangs on the wall by the sink. The room itself is very stark and practical, whitewashed from top to toe including the concrete floor, with plain larder

shelves and storage cupboards. The roller towel is the only print in the room and looks great against such a severe backdrop. I made it from a vintage linen curtain and then lined it with white towelling. There is also an old scrubbed pine kitchen table in the room used for chopping vegetables. The original turquoise blue paint remains on the legs, adding some more colour to the room.

Storage spaces

In the scullery I store all sorts of food in a glass-fronted cupboard. I was once given some herbs in a striped ticking bag, which gave me the idea of storing other food in bags. This is an excellent way to keep pulses and rice and bags are just as easy to use as storage jars. Label them by writing directly on to the bags or a sticky tape with a laundry marker pen. I used up all the pieces of blue, red and white stripes and checks that I had and they do look really pretty all together behind the glass.

The larder is also the place for keeping shopping bags and baskets. I keep my bread hanging up in a bag as the long loaves never seem to fit in the bread bin and the baskets are excellent for storing fruit and vegetables on the floor. I have made all sorts of bags in a traditional tote shape out of printed upholstery fabrics and have even made some

LEFT

An overall view of my

kitchen showing some

of my red and white

kitchenware.

The tablecloth is an old

curtain that has been

converted.

OPPOSITE

My carrier bag store
hangs on the back of
the larder door and
vintage tea towels line
up on the rail in front
of the cooker.

RIGHT

My favourite pepper
mill peaks out from
behind a china jug.

from old plaid wool blankets. They are all lined with canvas as they need to be strong if they are to be used to carry the shopping. They are much more practical than using plastic bags, which always seem to burst, and they can easily be washed now and then. I must have at least half a dozen and find they also come in handy as over-night bags. I have also lined some large wicker baskets to use as shopping bags.

Hanging from a hook behind the larder door is my carrier bag store. It is a tube of fabric with an elastic neck at the top and the bottom. You simply push the plastic bags into the top and then pull them out one by one from the bottom. They sell them in our village at local charity sales, which is where I copied the idea. I used to have a drawer in the kitchen that was bursting with bags and would never shut so I think they are the most brilliant idea. They also, with the right instructions, make excellent presents.

The other obvious present from the kitchen is home-made jam and marmalade. I am hopeless at making it so I cheat and buy it from the local market. It is easy to transform

This wicker basket had the roses attached when I bought it, but I added the floral lining to make it stronger.

Jam pots line up with their floral hats along the larder shelf.

33

the jars into gifts by making pretty fabric lids with a pair of pinking scissors. Rather than using string or an elastic band, bright-coloured hair elastics are great for attaching the fabric, and luggage labels are excellent for the gift tags. It is also easy to decant other foodstuffs such as biscuits or sweets into large glass jars and finish them in this way as presents.

Finishing touches

The other items I have collected in the kitchen are a wide variety of aprons. You can still find incredible old pinnies in thrift shops and they come in the most wonderful prints. My favourite one has different recipes for cocktails printed all over it and I once had a great one spelling out the calories of every conceivable food. They are often very kitsch but are good fun and amusing to collect. I also enjoy buying old cook books. Besides the recipes, they often have great illustrations and very funny cookery pictures of the strangest combinations of food – roast chicken decorated with glacé cherries or a 'log' of gammon and pineapple, for example! Cook books that are used regularly work well if they are covered in oilcloth or paper jackets as they can so easily be ruined. Aside from cooking I really enjoy spending time in my kitchen. We no longer have a sofa

OPPOSITE

This tablecloth with its 'sail boat' print has a rather Dutch feel that mirrors the painting behind. I have added a wide gingham border to the fabric.

35

RIGHT

The boot of my car –
full of groceries. The
shopping bags are
made from a mixture
of blankets and
printed linen. The
plastic one was a find
from Morocco.

and television in the room so now use our sitting room on a daily basis. But the stove gives the room a friendly feel and we still all congregate around the kitchen table. If I ever get bored of the blue, red and white colour scheme, it would be easy and inexpensive to change. The only item in the room that I would need to keep is the blue cooker as the rest cost very little.

I enjoy collecting all the old kitchen ware. There is nothing better than coming across a new item I haven't got – last week I found a red egg timer. The one rule I have when buying something is that it has to be practical. My collection is nearly at saturation point and I am tempted to sell all the red and start again. Perhaps I could go for green next time to mix with the blue. All I would have to do is paint the chairs again, find a few new tablecloths and tea towels, and I would have a brand new room! The possibilities are endless.

Extending the kitchen

Our hall is a fairly empty room with a large fireplace, stone-flagged floor and lots of book shelves. There are two wing chairs by the fire and a round table piled with books in the middle of the room. There is also an old refectory table, which sits against one wall with a couple of lamps on it and usually a big bowl of flowers.

I can use the refectory table as a sideboard and have a large circular table top that fits on to the round table to extend it. I cover the table with a giant felt tablecloth and then put a white cloth on top of this. I use a complete mixture of pairs of chairs from around the house. When I bother to make the effort it is wonderful to eat with the fire blazing on a cold winter's night. I have no wish to have a formal dining room as they always seem such cold rooms, only used for best occasions and rather out of date. Given the choice, I would rather combine a room such as a library with a dining room.

To tie in with all my different tablecloths I use lots of leftover fabric scraps, including tablecloth remnants, for napkins. I tend never to have the right amount in one design, so now have assorted piles – ready-made red checked napkins are mixed with ticking stripes and ginghams. For some strange reason I always end up with five rather than six of a set, just as one sock disappears in the wash. It doesn't matter if you have only enough fabric for the odd napkin as this can be used to line, say, a bread basket. Bias bindings also make lovely edgings on napkins and tablecloths. This cotton tape is available in the most incredible colours and looks great when the different binding colours are allowed to clash.

the kitchen

Storage bags

I made these bags from scraps of gingham or ticking, but you could just as easily use ready-made shoe bags. Each is made from a length of fabric sewn together up the sides. The top is then stitched down to make a channel into which lengths of cord are fed. I have stuck on linen tape for the labels and written on them with a marker pen. They are easy to pull off when you need to re-label the bags.

Collecting kitchenware

I started off by collecting red and white storage jars but now even have matching pots and pans. It is not always the patterns that match; often it is purely the colours. My one criterion for when I buy something for the kitchen is will I use it? I am just as likely to find something modern in the high street such as my striped mugs as I am a vintage jug in a junk shop.

Food covers

A friend made me this food cover out of
a piece of old 1950s kitchen fabric.
I particularly love the way that she has used
up an old broken necklace to weight the
edges. The beads look positively jewel-like
as well as being so practical. The ricrac braid
is also an easy way to finish off a small
circular hem as you don't have to turn over
the fabric, which can be tricky.

Napkins

Over the years, I have made up numerous
scraps of fabric into napkins and like to use
a combination of materials at any one
time. I tend to collect various red and white
tickings and checks but also have been
known to use the odd piece of floral or
pictorial fabric to add a touch of variety.
I also like to edge ready-made napkins
in contrasting bias bindings for a change.

the laundry

the laundry

I have always considered it the height of luxury to have enough space in a house to have a laundry room. For a long time I lived in a small flat where the ironing board doubled up as a desk top and I was forever having to hide piles of washing and ironing when friends visited. I dreamt of having a large airing cupboard with space for endless starched white sheets and lavender bags and of being able to hang an old-fashioned clothes dryer from the ceiling.

Then, quite recently, we moved house and at last I had inherited such a room. All too quickly, however, it was commandeered by my husband for his tool kit and vast range of car cleaning products. The only answer has been to build a large cupboard at the back of the room to hide all his clutter along with the hoover and mops. The rest of the laundry can now remain as clutter-free as possible.

Practicalities

Above all else, a laundry room has to be practical. Besides regular washing and ironing activities, such a room can be used for anything from boot cleaning to dog grooming. The entrance to my laundry is just by the back door and all the muddy boots seem to end up by the sink, so I have laid a blue lino floor, which is easy to keep clean. The walls and ceiling are painted with a shiny gloss white paint to withstand all the wear and tear and there is a high shelf around the room where numerous flower vases and pots are stored out of the way. Below it is a peg rail for hanging the ironed laundry.

The sink is under the window so I have made the curtains out of an old pair of striped beach towels – it doesn't matter if they get wet. They have been left unlined and just have ties at the top as opposed to curtain headings so they can be taken down and thrown in the wash. Bath or beach towels can also be a great find to convert into very practical and pretty bathroom curtains.

The laundry cupboard

At the back of the room is a large walk-in cupboard. I had a roll of floral paper left over from my last house which was just enough to paper the walls inside the cupboard. I love the cheerfulness of the very colourful print in an otherwise functional space and the contrast with the rather austere white walls of the rest of the laundry room. There are shelves from floor to ceiling on one side and another peg rail. Shelves like this are the perfect space for storing everything, from the car-cleaning kit to the tool box.

I used to keep all my sewing things in an old trunk and was forever rummaging to find what was needed. There are now so many

These haberdashery flowers are great for decorating all sorts of things, ranging from coat hangers to lavender bags. I keep my collection stored away in old glass jars.

43

ribbons and trimmings collected over the years, I can't bear to throw any away. Now, however, they are neatly sorted into a collection of old biscuit tins and glass jars and kept on a shelf in this cupboard, which is so much more practical.

Old wicker baskets are perfect for storing other items such as cleaning products, and a collection of old enamelware buckets really is great for all those messier items such as the shoe-polish kit. The peg rail at the back has become home to some of my endless shopping bags.

The airing cupboard

My actual airing cupboard has been built around the boiler. Because of the heat it generates, the panels on the doors are open so that the air can ventilate. To disguise the doors, I have covered them with lengths of antique toile fabric fitted on to stretchy wire at the top and bottom so it is easy to take them down and wash. The inside of the cupboard has then been finished with simple slatted shelves.

As well as storing sheets and towels and airing washing and ironing, the cupboard acts as a storage place for my large collection of antique quilts and blankets that have been gleaned over the years. Lavender bags and bars of scented soap tucked in between the

OPPOSITE

These lavender bags are very quick to make. Squares of fabric are hand-stitched together and tied like a parcel with a pretty ribbon.

the laundry

ABOVE

*Bars of soap lie
between my wool
blankets to help keep
the moths away.*

blankets keep the moths away – they not
only give off a wonderful smell to the room
as a whole, but are a great alternative to the
rather musty smell of mothballs.

Ways with fabric

I use up all sorts of scraps and ribbons to
make lavender bags. I even cut up old items
of clothing such as shirts and nightdresses.
I love hand sewing while watching television
and find it very therapeutic to run up square
parcels to fill with lavender. Each one is then
finished off with a ribbon tie. It is possible to

make piles of them in an evening and they
make great gifts as well as being useful
at home. I have got rather in the habit of
making them in squares but have in the past
made all sorts of different shapes and sizes –
rectangles and circles, both large and small,
are just as straightforward.

I have also begun to make a wide collection
of decorative coat hangers. I found some
wonderful knitted hangers in a local antique
shop and then began to play around with the
idea of making my own. I started with a scrap
of leftover fabric from the laundry cupboard

LEFT

These knitted coat hangers are a favourite of mine bought in my local market. I love the random choice of colours that are used in the stripes.

the laundry

RIGHT

My ironing board has a cover made from an old floral fabric. It is lined with a heat-resistant fabric and finally fitted with a draw string.

OPPOSITE

This peg bag hangs from a coat hanger on the washing line. The fabric is edged in bright pink bias binding.

the laundry

curtains, covering one and adding some old
hat flowers. I also covered some hangers in
a selection of brightly coloured silk lining
fabric and trimmed them with some tiny
fabric roses from a department store.
As well as using them in the laundry room
I leave hangers covered in this way hanging
out in a row on the peg rails in the guest
rooms instead of having a wardrobe, as
it leaves much more space.

Washing and ironing

One of my favourite things about living in
the country is being able to dry my washing
out in the fresh air on warm and – preferably
– windy days. There is nothing better than
the smell of freshly aired clothes. I now
have a hugely long washing line strung up
in our orchard.
One of the essential items for a washing line
is a peg bag and I made mine from a piece
of printed dress fabric. Cut out two pieces of
fabric the same shape. Trace the outline of
a wooden coat hanger for the top and then
make the bag so that it is narrower in the
middle so the pegs don't fall out in the wind.
Leave an opening on one side and edge
this with some bias binding for a neat and
colourful finish. A bag like this is easy to
make and could also be used as a good
general storage bag.

OPPOSITE

I used a leftover roll of wallpaper to brighten up my cleaning cupboard. I love the way this rather smart paper looks so out of context with the assorted contents.

LEFT

This favourite cup has been chipped so I use it to measure my soap powder rather than throw it out.

the laundry

RIGHT

This coat hanger was covered with a leftover scrap from the airing cupboard curtains and then trimmed with some vintage hat flowers.

OPPOSITE

My airing cupboard showing my sheets and blankets on a very tidy day!

When I had my small flat, the ironing board was always on show in the kitchen. I was horrified by the choice of covers available in the shops so I converted a wonderful old floral curtain into a cover and it became part of the decoration.

Ironing board covers are easy to make (see page 54) but it is important to be sure you use a flameproof lining. Trace the pattern from the old ironing board cover and finish it with a draw string so that it's easy to take off and wash each time you feel the need. Each time a cover wears out, it is simple to add a new one on top – the board gets more and more padded, too, which is particularly great for the ironing!

Now that I have a proper space for my laundry I am quite happy to spend hours in the wash room. In the winter, I find that it is the cosiest place in the house. There is nothing like the smell of lavender and clean washing mixed with the reassuring sound of the boiler striking up throughout the day. If only I had just that little bit of extra space I would install an armchair and even a television and really settle in.

the laundry

Ironing board cover

This ironing board cover is made from a piece of old cotton curtain fabric. It is lined with a heavy-duty flameproof curtain interlining and fitted with a draw string so it is easy to take off and wash. Use heavyweight cotton as this lasts longer and be sure that the fabric does not have any man-made content, which could be flammable. These covers are the top-selling item in my shop.

Useful ribbon ties

It is very practical to keep pairs of sheets tied together in my linen cupboard. It can be hard to tell which size sheets are once they are put away, so to save the bother of opening them up to find out, I use different-coloured ribbons to represent single or double when putting them away. Here I have used pale green and lilac ribbons and as long as they are loosely tied, the ribbons can be recycled.

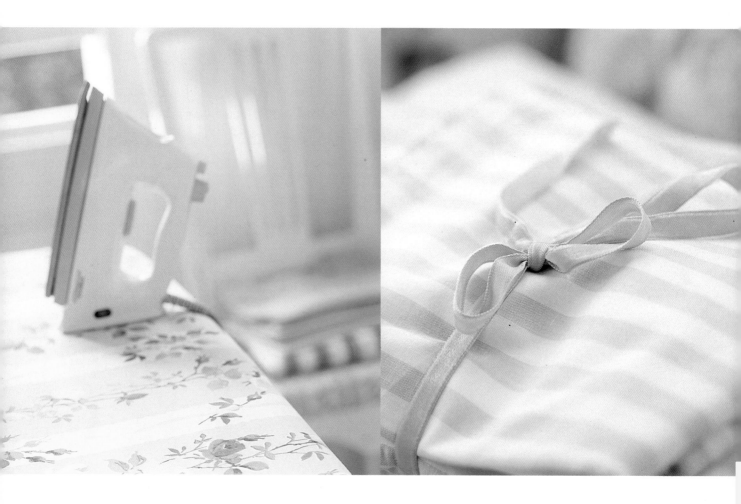

Decorative coat hangers

These decorative coat hangers make wonderful gifts and are simple to make. It's easiest to cover a coat hanger that is already padded. I pin the fabric so that its seam runs across the top, which can then be hand stitched. I have collected a wide range of haberdashery flowers to use as decoration. I tie the stalks to the base of the coat hanger and then tie a piece of ribbon over the top.

Lavender parcels

These lavender parcels are an excellent way of using up old scraps. I tend to use fabrics with mini-print designs in pastel colours and finish them off with scraps of clashing ribbons for the ties. It is worth buying the best quality filling as it lasts so much longer. Cheap lavender has often not been properly dried and has a tendency to go off and smell vile in no time.

the sitting room

the sitting room

RIGHT

*These children's chairs
fit well beside a
fireplace and can come
in handy as extra
seating. The pile of
books was a simple
way to add to the pink
theme of the room.*

My priority in decorating a sitting room is that it should be comfortable and have a friendly feel to it. Many homes these days have a cosy study that is used on a regular basis with the best room in the house left as the more formal sitting room. This only gets opened up for entertaining and as a result rarely looks lived in or has the charm of the other room. While I have two separate sitting rooms at home I have tried to use them both as much as possible. Inevitably, the room with the television wins over, but seriously comfortable armchairs and a big log fire do help to entice people next door.

Starting points

I am fortunate to have a fireplace in each room. I find it hard to decorate a sitting room without one and in the past have made a false chimney breast where one was missing in order to centre the room. I set about decorating the television room around the colours of a rather unusual old Turkish rug, in very strong reds and turquoises with yellow accents, which is large enough to fill most of the room. The walls were painted white and they remain so as I am still deciding whether to leave them or go for a colour. Some fairly bright contemporary paintings are the main feature in the room and they look good set against the plain whitewash for now.

The curtains are made out of inexpensive coarse yellow linen and they are edged with scarlet velvet – I like these two texture together. The curtains are a very simple shape, made with gathered headings on an antique curtain pole.

There is also a small side door into the garden from this room. It has a light printed curtain hung across it for when the room becomes too bright when the door is open in the summer.

Chair covers

Frequently the main choice that has to be made in a sitting room is how to cover the upholstered furniture. I already had two sofas and a couple of armchairs to use in the room. I have either inherited or bought them in antique shops and so they are all old. With a few exceptions, I much prefer to use old furniture as it is often beautifully made and has much more character than brand new pieces. Also it is often very much cheaper. I chose the pieces to use in this room strictly by their comfort factor.

The two sofas needed reupholstering rather than loose covering, so I chose the same yellow linen as the curtains for one and a faded red to go with the rug for the other. Because children and dogs use the room constantly and muddy paws often leave a

the sitting room

RIGHT

The pink and white colouring of the room even extends to a scrap of fabric on a matchbox.

OPPOSITE

An antique tablecloth is reflected in the mirror of this urban sitting room. The simple colour scheme helps to give the room a calm ambience.

the sitting room

trail over the furniture, I decided to cover the seat cushions with old fabric. I found a bright yellow velvet curtain at a jumble sale to tuck over the yellow sofa and have an antique paisley quilt strewn over the red one. These stronger colours would be too much for a whole cover but are great just for the seats. They are also easy to take off and clean and then throw back on again.

The armchairs were already covered in faded linens and although not ideal, work perfectly well for the time being with the decoration in the rest of the room. I have yet to decide what to cover them in, so to bring them in with the rest of the room, brightly coloured rugs are folded over the backs to add some colour. I have a feeling they may stay like this for some time!

Finally, there was one wing chair left and it needed a loose cover to disguise its rather sickly velvet upholstery. Some pink and red ticking went well, but there wasn't nearly enough. The answer was to patch the back with another fabric. Rather than try to match it, I used a clashing piece of Moroccan striped awning cotton.

Colourful cushions

The cushions are the main other decoration in the room. Old shawls make excellent covers – for this room I used some in red and

LEFT

The colours of this little painting are reflected in the sitting room itself.

OPPOSITE

Flowers make a huge difference in this sitting room. They add to the colour and prevent it from feeling too stark.

the sitting room

turquoise stripes, putting clashing fringes around the edge. An old red paisley shawl has also been cut up to mix with these. I had planned to have nothing floral but I relented when I came across two old sample pieces of fabric with a huge bunch of flowers on each piece. The colours were an uncanny match to the rest of the room. They are now made up with pink ticking borders similar to the fabric on the wing chair and sit in the centre of each sofa.

Bits and bobs

The rest of the room is fairly simple. A blue-painted washstand, which introduces more colour, is used as a side table, and one of my favourite things is a toy box of a similar blue that has a wooden cut-out frieze of dogs similar to my own terrier Stanley. I have converted it into a log box and it sits under another side table.

I tried to entice Stanley off the sofa – to no avail – by giving him a wonderful patchwork knitted blanket in his basket. I love these colourful throws and have recently started to collect them. The best place to find them is in junk shops and jumble sales.

The television takes up most of another table, again covered in a paisley quilt. It seemed pointless to make any attempt to hide it as it is the centre of attention in the room. Apart

LEFT

A view across my
television room in the
country. I have recently
begun collecting the
patchwork wool
blankets as seen in the
foreground.

67

RIGHT

*The back of this chair
has been covered with
a contrasting ticking
as I didn't have quite
enough fabric for the
whole chair.*

from a low, white-painted table, which is useful in front of the sofa, the rest of the furniture is made up of old wooden pieces, including a book shelf and simple side table, that I have acquired from various sources. In the summer, when the door is open into the garden and the sun streams in, this sitting room really is a riot of colour.

A more neutral setting

The sitting room next door has a wonderful big fireplace and flagstone floor. This has a much more wintry feel with lots of book shelves and darker furniture. Again, the room is whitewashed and here I shall definitely keep it that way. There is an old Dutch oil painting that hangs with early needlework pictures and some engravings that suit the simplicity of the plain walls. The window has such a pretty stone surround I am loathe to hang any curtains. The fireplace really is the best thing in here and we do spend plenty of time, particularly in the winter, sitting around a roaring fire.

The wall-to-wall book shelves form the major decoration in the room and even more books are piled high on a table behind the sofa. As time goes by I am quite sure that they will spill on to neighbouring chairs, but I don't think you can ever have too many books in a room. (I often choose paint colours from the colours of cloth books. They come in the most fantastic shades and it is much easier to take a book to the paint store and have the colour matched than it is to choose from a tiny swatch.)

Welsh blankets

The armchair that I wanted to use in this room has been covered in a patchwork of the darker shades of Welsh blankets. The leftover pieces have been used for some cushions. I made these by combining the plaids with some old black chintz, so they can be used either way round on the sofa. I also mixed the chintz with some old red ticking to add to the variety. The black floral fabric mixed with the plaids helps to prevent the room from being too serious.

Something a little airier

My sitting room in London is quite different again. It is a light space with a more modern feel. It is painted white, but here the floor is left with simple bleached floorboards and no rugs. The colour scheme, inspired by an old tablecloth, is simply pink, black and white. Once the colours had been decided on I was able to look out for things especially for the room – two pink children's chairs caught my eye in a junk shop and also a tiny scrap of pink and white toile came in handy to cover

the sitting room

RIGHT

*These colourful rugs
hang over the backs of
two armchairs while
I decide on their
upholstered covers.*

OPPOSITE

*This toy box was a
wonderful present as
the dog design on it
is similar to my beloved
terrier Stanley. It now
makes an excellent log
box in my sitting room.*

a matchbox. I have tried to leave the space fairly bare with very few pictures and not too much clutter and there are only white roller blinds at the window.

For the lighting I have found old white china table lamps with simple card shades or painted wooden candlesticks with white gloss paint and had them wired up. If I am having a party, I love to light the room with lots of candles, be they in antique candlesticks reflected by the mirror or tiny night lights dotted around the place. I also try and use the fire in this room as much as possible throughout the year.

I do hope that despite all the pink the room has an almost masculine feel. But should I ever change my mind, I know that it would be very easy and relatively inexpensive to change the colours.

I really enjoy being able to use these rooms. There is nothing like comfortably stretching out after a long Sunday lunch on the sofa with the newspapers or sitting by the fire chatting with friends.

With their plain white walls, minimal window treatments and natural flooring, these rooms have been simple to pull together – I have also had great fun looking for specific objects. As time goes by, items can then be changed or added, so I am glad that I am not too tied by anything I have done.

the sitting room

Extra seating

I use these kids chairs as side tables in the sitting room but as long as they are armless they can also come in handy for extra seating. They are easy to tuck away by the side of a fireplace and bring out in an emergency. Being old school chairs, they are easy to find in natural wood, but are quickly and readily transformed to whatever colour you choose with a plain coat of paint.

Clashing colours

I added this shocking pink bias binding to this striped cushion to cheer it up. The bow also acts as a practical closure. If I cannot find an exact match to something, I prefer to use a completely clashing colour instead. Trimmings and bindings are an especially easy way to do this. Bias bindings are great value for this purpose and are available in a huge range of colours and widths.

Patchwork blankets

I have recently started to collect these
fantastically colourful patchwork blankets.
They are easiest to find in charity shops
or flea markets and come in all shapes and
sizes. The best ones have crocheted edges and
wicked colour combinations. Besides using
them as the more conventional blanket
or throw they also convert into excellent
cushion covers or dog rugs.

Flowers

I could happily spend a fortune each week
buying flowers for the house but quite often
get away with buying just the cheapest of
the bunch. I try to mix together a few
clashing colours – say three shades of pink
or a jumble of orange and pink – and simply
pile them into a jug or vase. I do think they
make the whole difference to making a house
feel alive and lived in.

the bedroom

the bedroom

From a decorating point of view, the bedroom is my favourite room in the house. I have a passion for floral fabrics and old-fashioned rosy prints in particular and left to my own devices could happily use them throughout the house. The bedrooms are the one area where I feel I can really use these prints. I find there is a big difference between having a room that is pretty and fresh and somewhere that is too frilly and overly feminine and it is always a case of trying to strike a good balance.

My bedroom

My own bedroom is lilac, green and white. This colour scheme stemmed from an oil painting of mauve hydrangeas left to me by my aunt which I like very much. I also had a set of French engravings with old-fashioned green mounts. With these in mind I set out to look for material for the curtains. I already had a wonderful scrap of chintz printed with violets that was ideal, but there was only enough to make a couple of cushions. I searched everywhere for a new material to use but to no avail. So in the end, I had a fabric printed in the colourway of my own choosing. There are a few companies that will print their own designs to any colour for not much more cost than usual. This particular material now features large in the bedroom, appearing as curtains and on the bed head and valance.

I then painted the walls pale green, only to find the room looked rather gloomy. There can be a tendency with some old-fashioned floral fabrics for the room to end up looking like it belongs to a very old lady! In my case, I found that an old purple quilt helped to cheer it up but the walls needed changing. The end result is white panels over the green, leaving the colour in wide borders around the edges of the room. A purple wash line has been painted on the edge of the green bands. I am so pleased with how the white has lifted the room and with the way the panelling has worked that I have reproduced it in another room in a different colour.

Bed dressing

My favourite thing in the room is a giant patchwork blanket that I have made. Although it was easy to do, it took ages as I am really slow at knitting. I chose four colours for the wool to form a chequered pattern on the blanket and made each square about 15 cm (6 in) wide. Once the squares were knitted, they were quick to sew together and the sense of satisfaction once it was finished was immense. I have an aversion to duvets and like nothing better than linen sheets and old-fashioned

The colour scheme
for this bedroom
originated from the
oil painting of mauve
hydrangeas hanging
on the far wall. The
fabric on the bed
valance and curtains
was specially coloured
by a fabric
manufacturer to
match an old cushion.

the bedroom

OPPOSITE

A colourful silk lining and pale blue bobble fringe updates this vintage violet chintz.

LEFT

My knitted blanket in progress!

the bedroom

blankets. I prefer to use plain white linen in this room and have collected quite a lot over the years. It is easy to find pretty antique pillowcases decorated with lace but double sheets are more difficult. Plain sheets can, however, be transformed by sewing heavy cotton lace on to their edges.

Small details

The rest of the room is furnished quite simply. An antique mahogany chest of drawers and a laundry press prevent it from being too feminine, and an armchair is newly covered in a simple fresh green and white striped ticking.

The window seat is the only other area where there is more floral fabric. I have made up the cushions from the original piece of violet fabric and introduced some pale blue into the lilac and green colour scheme in the way of a couple of cushions and bobble fringe. It helps to inject some extra colour into a room, as if everything matches too closely it can look rather contrived. This said, I was delighted to be given my purple fluffy slippers and old-fashioned green radio to go in the room.

The rose room

For the spare bedroom I already had a bed covered in pink roses and some curtains to

RIGHT

A selection of my old feather eiderdowns. They can still be found in perfect condition with these pretty paisley covers.

OPPOSITE

A cosy pink hot-water bottle cover has been enlivened with scraps of lime green ribbon.

The delicate organza lampshade standing beside the bed was made by stitching the fabric carefully on to an old wire frame.

match left from my previous flat. I love this
material so was happy to decorate the room
around it. The walls are painted a faded
turquoise blue, a colour that I like very much
with pink. I then framed a number of
favourite Redouté rose prints in simple white
frames to hang in sets on the walls to break
up the expanse of blue.

Because this is a guest room I have fixed
up a peg rail for hanging any clothes on
rather than installing a wardrobe. It leaves
so much more space in the room. Some
pretty covered coat hangers are on the rail
to add to the decoration.

Old-fashioned bedding

Old-fashioned candy-striped cotton sheets
with matching pillowcases are on the bed.
These are a favourite of mine and are still
made these days in all sorts of colours.

A mixture of quilts and blankets is then piled
on top – there is an old-fashioned pale green
quilt with a pink lining for the bed cover
and a faded pink and green plaid throw for
the top blanket.

I love these vintage rugs that come from
Wales. They can be found in the prettiest
colours and are excellent for upholstery as
well as blankets. Several similar but different
ones upholster the bedroom chairs. They are
applied like patchwork with a different rug

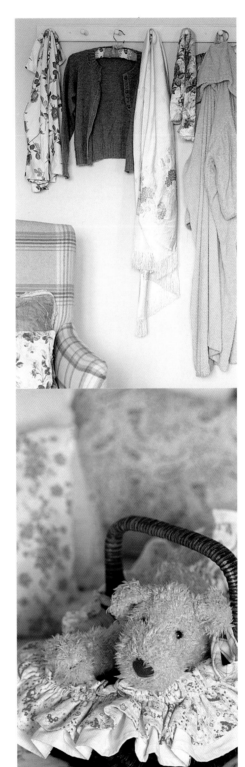

LEFT

*A peg rail acts as
an alternative to a
wardrobe in my spare
bedroom.*

BELOW

*I bought this basket
with the pretty lining
from an antique shop,
but the lining would
be easy to make.*

the bedroom

RIGHT

This old four-poster bed is made up with a mixture of antique white linen and paisley pillowcases. The chintz hangings are original, but the lining has been replaced with a glazed chintz stripe.

on the seat and arms. I love upholstering furniture in this way and would like to cover a whole sofa.

Blankets can be used in other ways too. Pillowcases can be made from small floral prints and then the leftovers used to edge bed blankets as a matching set. I also dye pretty antique sheets to match the fabric and then use them as bed covers. Old linen sheets take dye very well and it is fun to mix the pretty colours of the top and bottom sheets on the bed. They work best if they are made from pure linen and if they are dyed in pale pastel shades in the washing machine. New linen sheets are extremely expensive to buy but it is easy to pick up old ones in antique markets at a really good price.

Feather eiderdowns

I also love collecting old feather eiderdowns. They come in the prettiest faded paisley prints and really do keep one warm. It is hard to find them in good condition but they can successfully be cleaned in the washing machine and put through the tumble dryer, which often helps. However, check there are no holes first or you can end up with feathers everywhere.

The other option is to re-cover an old beaten-up eiderdown in a loose cover, making the equivalent of a duvet cover to fit and edge it with a small silk taffeta frill and ties. Some dry-cleaners will still re-cover eiderdowns in your own fabric, which is useful.

Adding a touch of freshness

In another spare bedroom, I have used some old paisley material that is similar to the eiderdowns. This room has an old four-poster bed with rose chintz curtains that I am really fond of as it is something I grew up with. The lining of the curtains was a rather dull beige print, but now it is a simple yellow striped cotton, which I find most cheerful. I have used the same stripe at the windows, edged with a pink bias binding.

By painting the room pure white – including the beams – and using white-painted furniture next to the mahogany bed, the space has been kept as fresh and light as possible.

Again, I have used heavy, lace-edged sheets and pillowcases on the bed with a pale Welsh blanket and an eiderdown on top. There are all sorts of pillowcases that I can use in this room. For example, I found some pretty dress-making fabrics in linen and brushed cotton that have made up well into covers. They look really pretty edged with haberdashery lace and are very easy to make. I mix them up with plain white or coloured linen sheets.

The window seat in my

bedroom has cushions

made from my

favourite violet fabric.

They are lined in lime

green silk and trimmed

with ice-blue bobble

fringe to add some

extra colour.

A small touch

I found it hard to find a good lampshade for beside the bed in this room so I re-covered an existing shade in striped organza. I gathered the fabric around the top of the frame and once this was stitched into place it was easy to attach to the bottom of the frame in the same way. To cover the stitching, I finished off the lampshade by sewing on a frill over both top and bottom.

Shapes of old lampshades often have far more character than the ones available now and it is easy to find them in junk shops. Even if they are covered in some hideous fabric, you can have them professionally re-covered in your own favourites.

Stylish variety

I have had such fun decorating these bedrooms. Although the formula for each room is similar, I have tried to give each one a completely different character. But above all, I hope the spare rooms are comfortable and hospitable for my guests. The beds are definitely warm and cosy with their blankets and eiderdowns and I make sure there is always a hot-water bottle ready on cool evenings and biscuits by the bed along with the clean linen sheets. I have one more room to do and maybe this time I shall decorate a bedroom without a floral print in sight.

LEFT

This linen cover was dyed green in the washing machine. The blanket is trimmed in the same print as the pillowcase.

OPPOSITE TOP

A pile of pillowcases are made from lightweight linen and dress-making lace.

OPPOSITE BOTTOM

This table is an old friend that I painted white especially for the bedroom.

89

the bedroom

RIGHT

*This armchair is
covered in vintage
blankets, similar to
others in the room.*

OPPOSITE

*The antique fabric
on the bed, the prints
and the postcards all
help to create the
'rose' theme in this
spare bedroom.*

the bedroom

Colour matching

While I have no wish to have a room that is colour coordinated from top-to-toe, I was very pleased to find these cosy pyjamas that matched my spare bedroom just perfectly. An object like a brightly coloured dressing gown hanging on the back of the door forms just as much of the decoration as anything else. It is these small points that can add so much to the finished effect.

Dress fabrics

This blanket had frayed edges so rather than dispose of it altogether, I have trimmed it with some printed cotton to hide the damage. I used the same print to make the pillowcases too, so they make a sort of matching bed set. It is easy to make floral print pillowcases from children's dress fabrics and they are often available in the softest lawn cotton.

Leftover wallpaper

Besides disguising my medical dictionary with a wallpaper jacket, I have found all sorts of other ways to use up leftover rolls and remains of rolls. I have lined my chest of drawers with different papers and covered old cardboard boxes for storage. It doesn't matter if each drawer has a different print, so even the shortest scrap of leftover paper can be used.

Blankets

It is easy to buy old wool blankets these days as so many people choose to use duvets instead. They are one of the best bargains in second-hand shops and good quality ones will usually wash well in the washing machine. There is nothing better than getting into a bed made up properly with a cosy blanket or two and newly laundered sheets smelling of fresh air.

the bathroom

the bathroom

One of my priorities when house hunting
was to have a bathroom with natural light
and I am fortunate to now have not just one,
but several, large windows in my bathroom.
In fact, the room is one of the largest in the
house, converted from what the previous
owners used as a master bedroom. It faces
on to the road and the smaller room at the
back was used as a spare bedroom with
the original bathroom tucked away on
a half-landing.

When we moved in, we felt it made sense to
have the bedroom at the back of the house,
which is much quieter and has a wonderful
view. So now the front bedroom has been
converted into a large bathroom and dressing
room and the half-landing room has become
a small spare bedroom.

Filling the space

As well as a big bath in the middle of the
room there was room for an entire wall of
built-in clothes cupboards to be built. Hidden
among them is a shower. The basin stands at
one end of the room set into an old
cupboard, which doubles up as a dressing
table. Opposite is the original fireplace, which
has been converted to gas. To add to the
feeling of space, two armchairs sit on either
side of the fireplace, one with a towelling
loose cover. This is a great place to sit and dry

This heavy cotton lace was simple to add to the plain white towels and is strong enough to withstand plenty of washing.

This last scrap of boat fabric was just enough for appliquéing on to a washbag.

*I really appreciate
the luxury of having
a fireplace in my
bathroom. The
armchair on the left
was re-covered in
towelling especially
for the room and is
now a great place to
sit and dry one's hair.*

LEFT

*These wooden shutters
keep out prying eyes
and they allow the
light to stream through
on a sunny day.*

OPPOSITE

*I am very fond of this
picture: a self-portrait
of my favourite great
aunt in the bath!*

one's hair by the fire. There is even room
for a pair of antique wardrobes and another
armchair at the other end of the room.
I could also fit in an old free-standing coat
stand, which I painted white and now use to
hang up the dressing gowns and towels.

Creating the atmosphere

The room is painted a cream-coloured off-
white and because it faces out on to the street
there are louvred shutters at the windows for
privacy. All the woodwork is painted a pale
shade of 'French' grey. I also have a collection

of Victorian seaside pictures with shell frames
I wanted to use but was concerned that using
shells to decorate the bathroom was a bit of
a cliché. I then came across some 1950s'
scenic boat fabric, which had a quite funky
feel to it. Through combining this with the
seaside pictures, it gave them more character.
As there wasn't much fabric I tried to make
the most of it, using it for cushions and a
squab seat. I had a baby deck chair that I
couldn't resist covering as well to add to the
seaside atmosphere of the room. Now it sits
comfortably by the fireplace. The leftover

the bathroom

pieces I then cut out and used as appliqué on some washbags.

I also had some vintage towelling with fishes printed on it which suited the room, so I made this into towels and flannels by edging it in bias binding. Rather than hang the pictures, they all sit stacked along the mantelpiece, mixed with a collection of colourful plastic mirrors from Morocco and a ship in a bottle. I love this room, particularly when the light is streaming in through the shutters and I can almost feel I am on holiday.

Introducing colour

The spare bathroom is painted white, including the floorboards, but it is a much more colourful room than the other one. I found an old piece of floral fabric with bunches of lilac, pink and yellow flowers on a fresh white background that I felt would suit the chairs in this room. It also conveniently matched a bright flower painting that I had, so I set about decorating the room around these colours.

There are some pink fluffy bath mats and all the spare coloured towels are stacked together on a green shelf unit which is useful for extra storage. I then found some heavy lace edging to trim the bath towels and some brightly coloured braid to decorate the linen hand towels. There are also some hand

LEFT

*This old 'boat' print
cushion cheers up the
kelim chair. Some
of these old pictorial
fabrics have a
wonderful humour
to them.*

OPPOSITE

*Emery boards sit on
the mantelpiece among
various ships.*

the bathroom

LEFT

The colours for this bathroom were taken from the floral print of the cushion fabric.

RIGHT

These luminous false flowers echo the painting hanging directly behind.

the bathroom

towels made from a floral printed linen, again edged with heavy cotton lace.

A vase of very false-looking flowers sits on the top of the shelves in front of the flower painting, which adds to the colour. Flowers can be fun if they look fake rather than trying to be real.

Finally, I gathered up a variety of glass jars and filled them with different-coloured bubble baths and cotton wool balls to fill the shelves. One large sweet jar is full of various coloured soaps. They come in such pretty pale colours that look good when they are grouped together and they also look good when they are put on a window sill with the light streaming through. The advantage of decorating a room like this is that the end result is bright and airy and it is very simple to put together.

Past reflections

I once had a very small flat and was able to make the bathroom out of a tiny room at the back which had a door opening out on to the garden. It was wonderful in the summer to have the door wide open with a great view on to the garden. Although I had to sacrifice the space I had used up by having a smaller kitchen, I felt it was well worth it. I feel very fortunate to have such a large and airy space for my present bathroom.

LEFT

*My collection of glass
bottles is grouped in
the bathroom and
filled with different
coloured bubble baths.*

OPPOSITE

*This floral print hand
towel is made from
an old furnishing
fabric and trimmed
with cotton lace.*

the bathroom

Hand towels

Old linen hand towels are easy to pick up but are often damaged where there is drawn thread work. This can easily be disguised by stitching a trimming over the top. Here I have used an embroidered edging, but ricrac or lace work just as well. I also like to make hand towels from old floral fabrics – the photograph on the previous page shows just one example, finished with some lace edging.

Washbags

All sorts of material can be used to make washbags so long as they can be washed. Here I used up some scraps of fabric as appliqué, hand stitching them on to a small zip purse. Draw string washbags are the easiest to make (rather like those featured in the kitchen on page 38) and if you choose the right fabric they can look great hanging from a bathroom shelf.

Glass jars

I have quite a mixture of old glass pots and bottles that I like to use in the bathroom. Huge glass sweet jars are handy for storing away the bath toys or makeup. A jam pot is perfect to fit cotton wool buds and old glass decanters look especially pretty when they are filled with different coloured bubble baths. Arranged in rows or groups on a shelf or windowsill they look wonderful.

Loo paper holders

I think that old waste-paper bins or baskets are just perfect for storing loo paper in the bathroom. I keep this particular old wire basket in my spare bathroom and ensure that it is piled high at all times with different coloured papers. Some people consider coloured loo paper to be the height of bad taste, but I love to see all those pastel colours mixed together!

children's rooms

I have such strong memories of my own bedroom as a child. My first room had pink curtains with a bobble fringe and fluffy white candlewick bed cover. I then progressed to pale blue walls and rosy printed curtains and finally was allowed up to the attic to make my own den. The excitement of being able to choose my own decoration was immense. It was a shrine to the Pony Club, rosettes proudly pinned up alongside pictures of my favourite show jumper. They were gradually replaced with the obligatory posters of pop stars and a lava lamp.

I was terribly envious of my friends who had duvets and Habitat furniture, as I slept in an old brass bed with an eiderdown. I now really appreciate the fact that my parents let me make my room into my own space from a fairly early age but were also able to guide me with their own taste.

Today's rooms

We have an attic in our house which is totally children's territory. There are two bedrooms and a miniature bathroom. The larger room belongs to my stepdaughter Jessica so has been decorated very much to suit her. It is really tempting for me as a decorator to want to make the room pretty and have it full of the floral fabrics and vintage toys that I love. I had to really edit my taste and try to choose

things to suit her rather than myself. I made sure she had the final say in my choice of materials and colours.

Jessica's bedroom

The starting point was when I found a length of old 1950s' kids' fabric, which Jess luckily liked. I used this for the curtains and as the fabric was quite narrow, bordered it with gingham. There was then enough left over to cover a toy box and make some cushions. The room had a lovely old painted door with glass panels, which I kept and simply covered the glass in the same fabric.

The bed sits across the room under the window and is now covered in a mixture of cushions so it can also be used as a sofa. I love brightly coloured woollen crochet blankets and have converted some into cushion covers. These are teamed up with old ticking stripes and checks. The bed has side curtains, which can be drawn right across, and they seem to be a never-ending source of entertainment for hide-and-seek. They are made from simple red gingham to match the border of the main curtains.

The desk in the room is an old side table covered in one of my oilcloth fabrics. This material is so practical and cheerful in children's rooms – it makes a perfect work top that is excellent for painting on and all

sorts of other mess. All the furniture is old in the room, picked up in junk shops and then painted in bright colours. I like the fact that nothing is too precious and it doesn't really matter if it gets broken.

The original pink wallpaper is still up and is soon to be changed. Jess has recently become quite a tomboy so it may be 'football' paper next, or we are thinking of painting an entire wall in blackboard paint, which she can then use as a drawing board. We may do graffiti all over the pink wallpaper before we repaint, which would be fun. There is red linoleum in the bathroom at present and I am considering replacing the bedroom carpet with more lino as it works so well.

The room next door

The other spare children's bedroom has been painted white with splashes of a big blue floral paper in the window frames and curtains to match. The main decoration is in the old-fashioned children's pictures all over the walls and in the bed linen, which is a mixture of floral printed duvet covers and quilts. There is another table covered in oilcloth, this time stapled over the top, which comes in handy as a changing table when any babies come to stay. There is also an old Moses basket that I had left from home which I had fun re-lining. I bought some

children's rooms

This upholstered child's
chair has a matching
cushion backed with
a bold striped cotton.

OPPOSITE

The toy box was
covered in the same
vintage children's
fabric with a dark
blue velvet base to
withstand wear and
tear. The desk has
an oilcloth tablecloth,
which is handy
for painting and
homework.

white flannel for the sheets and trimmed it with the same design as the oilcloth – that of a rosebud print – but in a different colourway. Putting different variations of the same print together can work well, so I made a new slip cover for the quilt in a third colour. I have used gingham again in this room. This time it is in the lampshades, to give some sense of continuity.

Making a den

The main play area is away from the house, over in our barn. There is an attic room above the stables which has yet to be restored, and I set it up as a playroom in an emergency one summer holiday. Most of the room was put together in a couple of days and it is so popular we have yet to change it. I love collecting old cowboy fabrics when I go to America, so this was an obvious place for me to use them.

The room has lovely old beams and rough brick walls, which made it easy to decorate. Some old 'Roy Rogers' woven curtains hang at the window and above the entrance. I also have all sorts of pieces of old scenic fabrics with farmyards and mountain views printed on them. They were perfect to make into pictures. Having measured the sizes of each image, I had some pieces of wooden board cut and then stapled the fabric over the top.

LEFT

This playroom has
been converted from
an attic room in our
barn. The wall and
floor have been left in
their original state.

OVERLEAF LEFT

Vintage 'Roy Rogers'
curtains hang at the
entrance as part of the
cowboy theme.

OVERLEAF RIGHT

It has been fun to
accessorise the room
with the occasional
stetson and cactus.

children's rooms

I was really pleased with the results once they were on the wall and this would be easy to do with all sorts of fabric. Any duplicate pieces are made into throw pillows.

An old sofa was perfect for the room, but it needed covering, so I made a blanket from red polar fleece. This is such great fabric for children. It is softer than cashmere, cheap and easy to wash. The edge of the cover is now bound in gingham and the corners are embroidered with gingham horseshoes to add to the Western theme.

I also had a length of material that had different cowboy themes depicted in patchwork squares. It was quite ugly as a piece, but the squares were great to use as cut-outs to make pillows. I cut out the different designs – stetsons in one, horses in another – and then stitched them on to white linen to make pillows. There is a great fabric you can buy in haberdashery stores which irons on to the back of fabric, sticking it down securely on to a base cloth. This makes it very much easier to then sew into place.

The finishing touches

A large table is covered in my favorite tablecloth with cowboys in action all along the border. I had enough space to set up a couple of beds in the room as well. These were old iron bedsteads from a school which

children's rooms

RIGHT

*A bold rose print
wallpaper is used
around the window
recesses. The rest of the
room is painted white.*

OPPOSITE

*An old kitchen table
has an oilcloth top so
it can be used as a
changing table.
The spare children's
bedroom is decorated
with old-fashioned
rose-bud fabrics and
vintage prints.*

I have painted bright red. I then added to the colour with some bright red blankets. A pretty red and white chest of drawers and some bright Lloyd loom furniture complete the setting. The rest of the furniture is quite rustic – an old garden table that worked as a desk and some garden chairs are dotted about the room for extra seating.

Children seem to love it in the barn. The cowboy decoration is really popular and I am surprised there aren't more contemporary fabrics with this theme. It is fun adding to the room by pinning up the odd old horseshoe or sitting a cactus plant on the window sill. Apart from the fact that it gets quite cold in the winter as there is no insulation yet, I really see no need to restore the room. The roughness of the walls and floorboards is part of its charm and the children can be as messy as they like as there is very little that can be ruined.

Looking to the future

In no time I am sure Jessica will want to decorate her room on her own, but for now I have had great fun organizing things with her advice! My own childhood bedrooms have had such an important influence on me. My love of rosy chintz, eiderdowns and many other things definitely stems from an early age. It will be interesting for me to see what kind of house Jess ends up with when she is grown-up.

children's rooms

Knitted toys

I love these old-fashioned knitted toys. They are often for sale in my local market and make great gifts for new-born babies. The patterns are still available in knitting shops, too, and it is also possible to find great designs for hand-knitted cardigans with motifs such as Scottie dogs. With a little planning, these patterns are easy to convert to knitted cushion covers.

Raffia embroidery

I bought this basket with the embroidery already applied, but raffia embroidery is, in fact, simple to do. Coloured raffia is quite easy to come by and simple designs can be quick and effective to create using a blunted embroidery needle with a large eye. I keep a look-out for old handy craft books as they often have good designs in them that are easy to copy.

Cut-outs

As an overall print, this cowboy fabric was rather ugly, but I thought that the emblems themselves would be perfect as cut-outs. When making the appliqué, it is easiest to buy an iron-on backing fabric that holds the material in place before overlocking the edges. I was able to make numerous variations of cushions from one short length of the original fabric.

Ottomans

Old ottomans are great as toy chests. Here I used an old velvet curtain to upholster the sides so that it would better withstand wear and tear. I decided to use the kid's print only for the top so that it will be less expensive to change when Jess grows up and will no doubt want something a little different for her bedroom. Gingham can make a good alternative to plain lining.

the home office

With the use of computers and modern technology I am able to spend an increasing amount of time working from home. As I commute between my shop and the house, my laptop computer now travels to and fro with me as a regular part of my baggage. I love the peace and quiet of working at home, particularly in the daytime, when I have the space to myself, and often escape from the hustle and bustle of my shop to concentrate on a project at home.

I used to just bring a pile of papers from the office and spread them out over the kitchen table, but I was always short of something, be it a sheet of stationery paper or a stapler. Now, however, with a certain amount of organising and very little expense I have been able to set up a proper office in the house. The room that I have converted into my workplace is our study. Because it is really an extension of the main sitting and entertaining room and used by all the family, I needed to retain its domestic atmosphere but somehow incorporate the efficiency of a proper office. The working fireplace has been kept and I use it constantly in the winter, sitting on one of a pair of leather club chairs situated on either side of it. I spend a good deal of time on research, browsing through books and magazines, and I reckon an armchair – if not a sofa – is vital for this. Some simple floor-to-

ceiling book shelves house some of my filing among the books and all in all this gives the room a very cosy atmosphere.

Creating order

I have made two work spaces in the room. One is an old desk with pigeon holes where I keep my post and paperwork. This tends to get fairly crowded with clutter. Under the desk is the filing system in stacks of box files, each covered in a different paper or fabric. I love mixing all the patterns together rather than having them matching.

Each box is used for a different subject, such as one for bank statements and one for the car documents, and each is instantly recognisable – the yellow stripy box, for example, is for house insurance. Filing like this is so much easier than in a proper filing cabinet as, if information needs to be taken elsewhere, the whole box can be carried around. Clothes pegs instead of paper clips are also good for tidying up paperwork and I keep a huge box of brightly coloured plastic pegs on the desk for this purpose.

For messages and notes I have a chalk board, painted red instead of black, propped up above the desk. It is just as practical as a blackboard and much less reminiscent of school. So long as the colour is fairly intense to ensure that the chalk is clearly visible,

OPPOSITE

This desk in the study is normally covered in mounds of paperwork. The 'red board' is a favourite of mine, as is the sculpture of the couple on the bench.

OVERLEAF

A pair of leather armchairs sit on either side of the fireplace. The wire racks (right) are excellent for storing my receipt books and stationery.

these boards look great in all sorts of colours. You just need to use an oil-based paint with a matt finish.

I also use an old wire post office rack for my filing and storage. This is excellent for stationery as the wire boxes are exactly the right size for foolscap paper and everything is clearly visible. Although my desk is always cluttered, the sight of all my writing paper and envelopes neatly stacked on the shelves along with the receipt books at least gives the appearance of an efficient work place.

Storage boxes and bags

Cardboard boxes can be a very functional form of storage. I have a pile stacked up by the armchairs. They are full of fabric samples but have somehow ended up doubling-up as side tables. They are very sturdy with lids and I ordered them from a professional packing and freight company. They come in all sorts of sizes and are incredibly cheap. I have left mine a natural cardboard colour but they would look very smart painted or covered in fabric as well.

And then there is my collection of vintage shopping baskets, gathered together over the years. There are many different kinds available, but in particular I look out for the wicker ones with brightly covered plastic handles. They are invaluable for storage all

the home office

over the house – but especially useful in the
office. Pencils and crayons are stored in one
and staplers in another. They are also
excellent for storing CDs and videos.

A more versatile work place

The other desk space is set across the room.
I like working in the natural light as much as
possible so set up a table close to the window.
A telephone point has been installed there
together with a bank of plugs to service the
area and I try to keep the table top free of
clutter so there is plenty of space to work.
The desk itself is really an old kitchen table.
I chose it because it has an adjustable top
and is not too work-like. It extends when
I need to spread myself out, but normally it is
kept folded down as there isn't too much
space to spare. The top is made of scrubbed
pine so it can be bleached and cleaned and is
hard-wearing. It is impervious to the hot
mugs of coffee and tea needed to entice me
to work. I keep the computer printer
underneath this table where it is pretty much
out of sight but convenient to use. All I have
to do is plug in my laptop and I am set up.
The book shelves behind are extremely
useful. I keep all sorts of practical reference
books there. The ones that I use a lot are
bound in different fabrics and papers.
I began by covering the telephone directories

This kitchen table is excellent as my work station. It has an extending leaf and the scrubbed pine top is impervious to my endless coffee mugs. The telephone book in the foreground has been covered with one of my wallpapers.

the home office

RIGHT

I have painted my chalk board red instead of black for a change.

OPPOSITE

Old cloth books are often the most wonderful colours. I have collected them over the years to make my own colour chart for design work.

and then have moved on to such items as my address book, message book and atlas. It has become quite a habit! Not only are they so easily identifiable in this way, they also withstand much more wear and tear. I use up old scraps of wallpapers and fabric and stick them on with spray glue. Simply cut out a piece of fabric or paper slightly larger than the book, coat the back with the glue and stick it on to the cover. Then trim the fabric or paper to the right size, cutting around the edge of the book. Plain note books can be transformed in this way, particularly if you use rather grand antique fabrics such as velvet or damask, and they are excellent as gifts.

Keeping track

An oil painting was hanging over the fireplace but I have replaced it with a large notice board. I find these incredibly practical in a work place for pinning up all sorts of things from lists and photos to stamps and even the odd cheque waiting to be banked. It has been made from a large piece of pin board, which I then wrapped in tin foil. A grid of black elastic stretches over the top, stapled down where the lines cross. I tried to make the board as decorative as possible and began by pinning up old prints and family photographs. The tin foil is now only visible in small chinks around the paperwork, but when the afternoon

Versatile storage. This giant pin board has been wrapped in tin foil and then covered in a grid of black elastic. It began as a family photograph board but has slowly been taken over by office filing. The wire baskets are great for larger objects.

sunshine floods into the room the light is beautifully reflected from it. As time goes by, more and more layers are added to the board so that it has become rather like an old friend. I would like to have my office at work entirely lined in pin board and whitewashed from floor to ceiling.

The importance of versatility

Now that I have my study set up properly I love working at home. The most important thing has been to have plenty of adaptable storage space and a good clear desk top. Apart from the book shelves I have made sure all the furniture is free-standing.

It is very tempting to build a fitted desk space with custom-built shelves for the computer and printer. My experience of this is that it never works. Not only is it expensive to do, but inevitably requirements change. The computer is traded for a larger one and the filing space is never big enough.

My office looks much more like a sitting room than a work space but is, in fact, incredibly efficient to work in. As time goes by, I shall put more pictures on the wall, collect even more box files and baskets, and my pin board will groan under the weight of added clippings and notes. I love the way this room can adapt from being a hive of activity during the day to a cosy sitting room in the evenings.

the home office

Chalk boards

Chalk boards work in all sorts of colours
besides black as long as the shade you choose
is dark enough so that the white writing
shows up on it. It is important, too, to use an
oil-based paint so that the board can be
washed down now and then. It must also
have a flat matt finish or else the chalk will
slip and slide across the surface and the
powder won't adhere especially well.

Vintage fabrics

I love these vintage abstract fabrics but I can
often only find short lengths these days.
They are becoming increasingly collectible so
I am careful not to cut them up to make such
small items as cushion covers or napkins.
These sort of prints can look great once they
are simply framed on a plain canvas stretcher
and hung on the wall alongside
contemporary paintings.

Filing

For filing, I use piles of storage boxes instead of a filing cabinet as they are much more portable when I work between my home and the office. I keep them stacked up under my desk and try to have each one in a different print so that they are easily recognisable. I now know at a glance which is, say, car insurance or the holiday file, and I don't have to search for the label.

Pinboard

My pinboard has evolved into being a part of my filing system. It is the perfect place to keep my stamps, for example. It began as a plain board but I added the silver foil to brighten it up and then the elastic grid. It is so much more practical to be able to tuck things in behind the tape rather than having to always find a drawing pin. They are never there when you want them.

index

index

author's acknowledgements

So many people have helped me on this project in either a practical way or with their encouragement and support, but in particular I would like to thank Sue Thompson, Angela Vernon, Eva Philipson, Eileen Tyndall, Mrs Noor, Mark Parr and Tony Crawley for all their incredible handywork. Harriet Beauchamp, Jody Kerr, Yvette Masters, Alice Elliot, Sarah Taylor, Nesta Fitzgerald and Gill Hicks for all their support and hard work at the shop. Pia Tryde for her wonderful photographs and for being such an inspiration to work with. Georgina Rhodes, Catherine Bradley, Emma Callery and Denise Bates for all their help, patience and vision. Camilla Lowther, Kevin Kollenda, David Macmillan and Julian Alexander for their help. Jo and Millie for putting up with all the mess when we were working at home. Sarah Landeg who has been the most supportive assistant I could have wished for. Above all, Hugh and Jess for putting up with me while I worked on this project.